PRESENTED TO:

_____

Prayer takes place in the heart,
not in the head.

Carlo Carretto

PRESENTED BY:

_____

Life's Daily Prayer Book for Women:
Prayers to Encourage and Comfort the Soul
©2004 Elm Hill Books
ISBN: 1-404-18517-8

The quoted ideas expressed in this book (but not scripture verses) are not, in all cases, exact quotations, as some have been edited for clarity and brevity. In all cases, the author has attempted to maintain the speaker's original intent. In some cases, quoted material for this book was obtained from secondary sources, primarily print media. While every effort was made to ensure the accuracy of these sources, the accuracy cannot be guaranteed. For additions, deletions, corrections or clarifications in future editions of this text, please write ELM HILL BOOKS.

Manuscript written and compiled by Vicki J. Kuyper in association with Snapdragon Editorial Group, Inc.

LIFE'S Daily Prayer BOOK

for Women

Prayers to Encourage and Comfort the Soul

Elm Hill Books
An Imprint of J. Countryman®

Introduction

An old hymn goes: "What a friend we have in Jesus, all our sins and griefs to bear. What a privilege to carry everything to God in prayer." They're wonderful words, aren't they—comforting, strengthening, liberating. And they are words of truth! In the Bible, God invites us to friendship with Him, a friendship that urges us to cast all our cares on Him.

Life's Daily Prayer Book for Women was designed to guide and inspire you as you reach out to God in friendship and converse with Him concerning the issues, activities, and relationships that define your life. Think of these written prayers as letters to your best friend— God. Make them your own by adding the names of family and friends and specific needs. And don't forget to record and date your answers. May God bless you as you embark on this exciting spiritual adventure.

Life's Daily Prayer Book for Women
Prayers to Encourage and Comfort the Soul

Lord, the newness of this day
Calls me to an untried way:
Let me gladly take the road,
Give me strength to bear my load,
Thou my guide and helper be—
I will travel through with Thee.

Henry van Dyke

Daily Prayers ...

# Daily Prayer ...
for salvation

*God so loved the world that he gave his only
Son, so that everyone who believes in him
will not perish but have eternal life.*

John 3:16 NLT

Dear Heavenly Father,

I know now that there has never been a time when You
didn't love me—from inside my mother's womb, right
up to this moment. Despite my selfish mistakes, I'm a
precious daughter in Your eyes. Help me now as I strive
to become the daughter You created me to be.

I'm sorry for the times I've chosen to go my own way,
following paths that led me away from You. Please
forgive me. I know Jesus paid for those choices with
His life. And now I not only walk away free but I've
been given the opportunity to spend eternity in Your
presence. Words could never express the depth of my
gratitude for this incredible gift. Thank You.

Amen.

*Being sorry in the way God wants makes a person change his heart and
life. This leads to salvation, and we cannot be sorry for that.*
2 Corinthians 7:10 NCV

MY PERSONAL PRAYER

The essential fact of Christianity is that God thought all men worth the sacrifice of his Son.

William Barclay

Dear Father:

_____

_____

_____

_____

_____

_____

Amen

Whoever calls on the name of the LORD will be saved.
Joel 2:32 NKJV

The "right time" is now. The "day of salvation" is now.
2 Corinthians 6:2 NCV

Daily prayer ...

for peace

Do not worry about anything, but pray and ask God for everything you need, always giving thanks. And God's peace, which is so great we cannot understand it, will keep your heart and minds in Christ Jesus.

Philippians 4:6, 7 NCV

Dear Heavenly Father,

I long for Your peace in my heart, a place of quiet trust where I can rest in the knowledge that You truly do make something good come from every circumstance.

I know that You not only see but also care about every detail of my life. Right now, those details seem tangled into a knotted mess. Please take every anxious thread, every tightly pulled knot of uncertainty, sorrow, conflict, and disappointment into Your gentle, loving hands.

Untangle my emotions. Sort out my jumbled thoughts. Calm my restless spirit. Help me experience Your supernatural peace in a real and tangible way.

Amen.

God causes everything to work together for the good of those who love God and are called according to his purpose for them.

Romans 8:28 NLT

MY PERSONAL PRAYER

*O God, make us children of
quietness, and heirs of peace.*
Clement of Rome

Dear Father:

—————————————————————

—————————————————————

—————————————————————

—————————————————————

—————————————————————

—————————————————————

—————————————————————

Amen

*Mercy and truth have met together;
righteousness and peace have kissed.*
Psalm 85:10 NKJV

Because of Christ we now have peace.
Ephesians 2:14 NCV

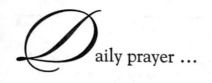 aily prayer ...

for wisdom

> *If any of you lack wisdom, you should pray to God, who will give it to you; because God gives generously and graciously to all.*
>
> James 1:5 GNT

Dear Heavenly Father,

Your ways are wise, as well as loving, and I want to be more like You—a woman of wisdom, not just intelligence. Show me how to put what You've taught me into practice in my life, to wisely apply what I know to what I do.

Help me, Lord, to see situations in my life—both good and bad—as you see them, in light of eternity. Give me the grace to speak wisely to others. And grant me the courage to walk in all Your ways, which is the wisest pursuit of all.

I want to be wise in Your eyes, Lord. Show me how.

Amen.

> *The wisdom of this world is foolishness to God. As the Scriptures say, "God catches those who think they are wise in their own cleverness."*
>
> 1 Corinthians 3:19 NLT

MY PERSONAL PRAYER

*Knowledge is
the power of the mind,
wisdom is the power of the soul.*
Julie Shannahan

Dear Father:

_____

_____

_____

_____

_____

_____

Amen

*Cling to wisdom—she will protect you.
Love her—she will guard you.*
Proverbs 4:6 TLB

*The Lord's rules can be trusted.
They make plain people wise.*
Psalm 19:7 NCV

Prayers to Encourage and Comfort the Soul   15

aily prayer ...

for joy

> *I have God's more-than-enough, more joy in*
> *one ordinary day than they get in all their*
> *shopping sprees.*
>
> Psalm 4:6, 7 MSG

Dear Heavenly Father,

I get so wrapped up in trying to create a happy life for myself and those I love. I know I'm told that the pursuit of happiness is my "inalienable right," but I want to be more concerned about my "pursuit of God," my desire to better know You—the only real road to joy, to a depth of delight that doesn't disappear when things go wrong.

When happiness is hard to come by, help me learn to draw more consistently on this wellspring of joy. Help me delight in the little gifts You bring my way every day ... a child's hug, a friend's smile, and the fact that You hear my every prayer.

Amen.

> *Jesus said, "I've told you these thing for a purpose:*
> *that my joy might be your joy, and your joy wholly mature."*
> John 15:11 MSG

MY PERSONAL PRAYER   *Joy is the echo of God's life in us.*
Joseph Marmion

Dear Father:

_____

_____

_____

_____

_____

_____

_____

Amen

I will rejoice in the LORD,
I will joy in the God of my salvation.
Habakkuk 3:18 NKJV

In your presence there is fullness of joy; in your right hand
are pleasures forevermore.
Psalm 16:11 NRSV

aily prayer ...

for justice

> *The LORD is your mighty defender, perfect
> and just in all his ways; your God is faithful
> and true; he does what is right and fair.*
>
> Deuteronomy 32:4 GNT

Dear Heavenly Father,

You've woven a longing for justice into my human heart. When I read the paper or watch the news, I often feel emotions of grief and anger rising to the surface. When my family is treated unfairly or someone judges me before knowing the whole story, I want to see justice done.

Remind me to rely on You for that justice. Guard my heart from bitterness, anger, or revenge—even if I only entertain them in my mind. Only You are righteous. Only You are truly just. Only You know the whole story—the eternal story. Only You have the power to set things right, once and for all.

Amen.

> *He will make your righteousness shine like the dawn,
> the justice of your cause like the noonday sun.*
>
> Psalm 37:6 NIV

MY PERSONAL PRAYER

The pearl of justice is found
in the heart of mercy.
Saint Catherine of Siena

Dear Father:

_____

_____

_____

_____

_____

_____

Amen

Your throne is founded on two strong pillars—
righteousness and justice.
Psalm 89:14 NLT

Justice is a joy to the godly.
Proverbs 21:15 NLT

Prayers to Encourage and Comfort the Soul   19

Daily prayer ...

for comfort

Oh, love me—and right now!—
hold me tight! Just the way you promised.
Comfort me so I can live, really live;
your revelation is the tune I dance to.

Psalm 119:76, 77 MSG

Dear Heavenly Father,

I know what it's like to comfort a child you love, to hold him or her close and listen through tears to whatever tragedy—big or small—has taken place. But right now, I'm the child, and my heart is breaking.

Hold me in Your arms. Listen to the ache that's in my heart. Dry my tears from the inside with a touch of Your tender, loving hand. I need to know You're near and that You care. Gently remind me that You have the power to heal every hurt and help me make it through what I'm facing right now. As your beloved daughter, I long to feel a daddy's love, to find a safe place close to Your heart. Draw me near.

Amen.

Sing, O heavens! Be joyful, O earth! And break out in singing,
O mountains! For the LORD has comforted His people,
and will have mercy on His afflicted.

Isaiah 49:13 NKJV

MY PERSONAL PRAYER

*God does not comfort us
to make us comfortable,
but to make us comforters.*

John Henry Jowett

Dear Father:

_____

_____

_____

_____

_____

_____

Amen

*Thus says the Lord: As one whom his mother comforts,
so I will comfort you.*
Isaiah 66:13 NKJV

*I call to you in times of trouble,
because you answer my prayers.*
Psalm 86:7 GNT

Prayers to Encourage and Comfort the Soul   21

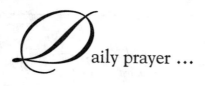# Daily prayer …

for forgiveness

Dear Heavenly Father,

There's nothing else to say but "I'm sorry." I know we've been down this road before. My heart wants to promise perfection. I want to believe that this is the last time I'll ever blow it. But, that isn't the reality of my life. Every day is a battle. I struggle between following You and choosing what feels right at the moment. I need Your wisdom and power to persevere toward a true change of heart and action. But, most of all, I need Your forgiveness.

Thank You for asking Jesus to pay the high price for what I've done. The thought of His sacrifice and Your unending grace humbles me beyond words. "Thank You" will never be enough.

Amen.

MY PERSONAL PRAYER

Humanity is never so beautiful as when praying for forgiveness, or else forgiving another.

Jean Paul Richter

Dear Father:

_____

_____

_____

_____

_____

_____

Amen

God has purchased our freedom with his blood and has forgiven all our sins.
Colossians 1:14 NLT

You, LORD, forgive us, so that we should stand in awe of you.
Psalm 130:4 GNT

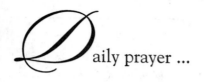

Daily prayer ...

for protection

Jesus said, "Holy Father, I am no longer in the world. I am coming to you, but my followers are still in the world. So keep them safe by the power of the name that you have given me."

John 17:11 CEV

Dear Heavenly Father,

The world is a frightening place. I look around me and see endless opportunities for disaster and tragedy. And yet, I place my trust in Your promise to send Your angels to watch over and guard me.

I know, Lord, that risk and pain are part of this world. I can't hope to escape every unpleasant circumstance. Just the same, I commit myself to Your boundless love. I will trust in You, whatever comes. Protect me in the way You see fit, in the way that best advances Your purpose for my life.

Amen.

This God—how perfect are his deeds, how dependable his words!
He is like a shield for all who seek his protection.

2 Samuel 22:31 GNT

MY PERSONAL PRAYER

The center of God's will
is our only safety.
Betsie ten Boom

Dear Father:

_____

_____

_____

_____

_____

_____

Amen

The Lord will deliver me from every evil attack
and will bring me safely to his heavenly Kingdom.
2 Timothy 4:18 NLT

God orders his angels to protect you wherever you go.
Psalm 91:11 NLT

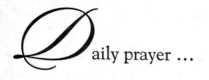 **aily prayer ...**

for courage

> *Wait on the LORD; be of good courage, and*
> *He shall strengthen your heart; wait, I say,*
> *on the LORD!*
>
> Psalm 27:14 NKJV

Dear Heavenly Father,

Like a child hiding behind her mother's skirt, I stand behind You. When it comes to courage, I have none of my own. Without You, I would be filled with fear, terrified of a future I cannot see.

Thank You for patiently taking my hand and helping me face my fears. Knowing You're there, knowing You have a plan—and that I am an integral part of it—gives me the courage to step up to the line and become the person You created me to be—a person who won't falter, won't shrink back, and who won't lose out on the great blessings You have prepared for my life.

Amen.

Be strong and courageous. Do not be terrified; do not be discouraged,
for the LORD your God will be with you wherever you go.
Joshua 1:9 NIV

MY PERSONAL PRAYER

*Courage is fear
that has said its prayers.*
Dorothy Bernard

Dear Father:

_____

_____

_____

_____

_____

_____

Amen

*Be firm in your faith. Stay brave and strong.
Show love in everything you do.*
1 Corinthians 16:13, 14 CEV

*I, the LORD your God, will hold your right hand,
saying to you, "Fear not, I will help you."*
Isaiah 41:13 NKJV

Prayers to Encourage and Comfort the Soul   27

Daily prayer ...

for strength

*I can do everything with the help of Christ
who gives me strength.*

Philippians 4:13 NLT

Dear Heavenly Father,

Though Your strength is limitless, it's tempered with wisdom and gentleness. You are both my strong tower and my tender, loving Father. Help me to find that proper balance of gentle strength in my own life.

Physically, I need the strength to persevere, pressing on with my responsibilities, even when demands on my time and energy are high. Emotionally, I need the strength to be honest about what's going on inside, without making excuses or letting my feelings take the lead. Spiritually, I need strength enough to stand strong in my faith without wavering, to hold my heart constantly open to hear Your still, small voice guiding and directing me.

Amen.

*How hard it is to find a capable wife! She is worth far more than jewels!
... She is a hard worker, strong and industrious.*

Proverbs 31:10, 17 GNT

MY PERSONAL PRAYER

Father, hear the prayer we offer,
not for ease that prayer shall be,
but for strength that we may ever
live our lives courageously.

Love Maria Willis

Dear Father:

_____

_____

_____

_____

_____

_____

_____

Amen

The joy of the LORD makes you strong.
Nehemiah 8:10 NIrV

In quietness and confidence is your strength.
Isaiah 30:15 NLT

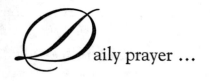 aily prayer ...

for rest

The LORD is my shepherd; I have everything
I need. He lets me rest in fields of green grass
and leads me to quiet pools of fresh water.
He gives me new strength.

Psalm 23:1–3 GNT

Dear Heavenly Father,

I'm a sheep in need of a Shepherd. Right now, I'm
picturing those green fields You spoke of. I long to lie
down in the supple blades of grass, to soak in the
warmth of the sun, and hear the babbling of a brook
gently winding its way to the still, quiet pool of Your
presence. I need Your refreshment and peace.

But, most of all I need rest: rest from my schedule, rest
from the demands of my family, rest from "doing" to a
place of simply "being."

Lead me to that place. Calm my mind and my emotions
so I can slow down enough to find real rest. Lead Your
little lamb to where she needs to be.

Amen.

Jesus said, "Come to me, all of you who are weary
and carry heavy burdens, and I will give you rest."
Matthew 11:28 NLT

MY PERSONAL PRAYER

*Jesus knows we must come apart
and rest awhile, or else we may
just plain come apart.*

Vance Havner

Dear Father:

_____

_____

_____

_____

_____

_____

Amen

My Presence will go with you, and I will give you rest.
Exodus 33:14 NKJV

*Those who rest in the shadow of the Most High God
will be kept safe by the Mighty One.*
Psalm 91:1 NIrV

Prayers to Encourage and Comfort the Soul   31

Daily prayer ...

for hope

My prayer is that light will flood your hearts
and that you will understand the hope that
was given to you when God chose you.

Ephesians 1:18 CEV

Dear Heavenly Father,

You are my hope in an often-hopeless world. You are my hope of heaven, my hope of peace, my hope of change, purpose, and unconditional love. Fill the reservoir of my heart to overflowing with the joy that real hope brings.

Let me see beyond my present circumstances to a place where Your goodness will be revealed. Help me cling patiently to hope as I wait for Your perfect timing, even when my human heart cries out for relief "now." Show me how to continue to hope, even when I don't understand all of the "whys." Again today, I affirm that my hope comes from no other one, no other place—only from You.

Amen.

May the God of green hope fill you up with joy, fill you up with peace,
so that your believing lives, filled with the life-giving energy
of the Holy Spirit, will brim over with hope!

Romans 15:13 MSG

MY PERSONAL PRAYER

*Hope is the struggle of the soul,
breaking loose from what is perish-
able, and attesting her eternity.*
Herman Melville

Dear Father:

_____

_____

_____

_____

_____

_____

Amen

I wait quietly before God, for my hope is in him.
Psalm 62:5 NLT

*Be alert and think straight. Put all your hope in how kind
God will be to you when Jesus Christ appears.*
1 Peter 1:13 CEV

Prayers to Encourage and Comfort the Soul   33

 aily prayer ...

for patience

> *The LORD is a God of justice. Blessed are*
> *all who wait for him!*
>
> Isaiah 30:18 NIV

Dear Heavenly Father,

It takes nine months for a child to grow and mature in a mother's womb. The name of the game is patient waiting. But at least there is some understanding of what a mother's pregnancy entails, what is to be gained, and approximately how long the wait will be. Right now all I know is that I'm waiting for something, though I'm not sure what, to fully develop and mature.

Teach me patience as I wait—the patience that comes from putting my confidence in You and Your perfect timing. When my frustration begins to build, remind me of Your sovereignty and goodness. Help me to let go of my own agenda and fully accept Yours, knowing that the outcome is in Your hands.

Amen.

Be brave. Be strong. Don't give up. Expect GOD to get here soon.
Psalm 31:24 MSG

MY PERSONAL PRAYER

Obedience is the fruit of faith;
patience, the bloom on the fruit.
Christina Rossetti

Dear Father:

_____

_____

_____

_____

_____

_____

Amen

I was patient while I waited for the LORD.
He turned to me and heard my cry for help.
Psalm 40:1 NIrV

When the way is rough, your patience has a chance to grow.
James 1:3 TLB

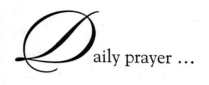

Daily prayer ...

for contentment

*Satisfy us in the morning
with your unfailing love, so we may sing
for joy to the end of our lives.*

Psalm 90:14 NLT

Dear Heavenly Father,

It seems like I'm always longing for things I don't have, things I don't need, things that would serve little or no purpose in my life. I let what I don't have define me. If I had a better nose, I'd be pretty. If I had a better personality, I'd have more friends. If I had more money, I'd be happy. Forgive me spurning the way You created me and the blessings You've placed in my life.

I want today to be the first day of my new life—a life filled with appreciation and contentment. Starting right here, right now, I declare my thankfulness for the blessings You've placed in my life, and I choose not to compare myself to others.

Amen.

I have learned to be satisfied with what I have. I know what it is to be in need and what it is to have more than enough.

Philippians 4:11, 12 GNT

MY PERSONAL PRAYER

*It is so important not to waste
what is precious by spending
all one's time and emotion on
fretting or complaining over what
one does not have.*

Edith Schaeffer

Dear Father:

_____

_____

_____

_____

_____

_____

Amen

*Stay away from the love of money;
be satisfied with what you have.*
Hebrews 13:5 NLT

*He satisfies the longing soul,
and fills the hungry soul with goodness.*
Psalm 107:9 NKJV

Prayers to Encourage and Comfort the Soul

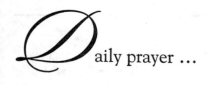

Daily prayer ...

for faith

What is faith? It is the confident assurance that what we hope for is going to happen. It is the evidence of things we cannot yet see.

Hebrews 11:1 NLT

Dear Heavenly Father,

I believe in You. I have no doubt that You are alive and present in my life, watching over my every step. I know that if I died today, I would spend eternity with You. But, Lord, I want my faith to accomplish more than a blessed outcome. I want the kind of faith that trusts You in the everyday matters of life, the kind that addresses the difficult questions and the nagging doubts.

I'm sure that kind of faith doesn't come easily. It means that I must place myself in Your care minute by minute. It means that with each challenge, I must choose to rest in Your sovereign wisdom and divine understanding. Give me the grace and courage, Lord, to become a true woman of faith.

Amen.

We walk by faith, not by sight.
2 Corinthians 5:7 NKJV

MY PERSONAL PRAYER

Belief is a truth held in the mind.
Faith is a fire in the heart.
Joseph Fort Newton

Dear Father:

_____

_____

_____

_____

_____

_____

Amen

Because of our faith, God has brought us into this place of
highest privilege where we now stand, and we confidently and
joyfully look forward to actually becoming all that God has
had in mind for us to be.
Romans 5:2 TLB

Jesus said, "All things are possible to him who believes."
Mark 9:23 NKJV

Prayers to Encourage and Comfort the Soul

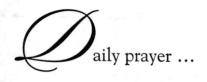# Daily prayer ...

for perseverance

*Let us run with endurance the race that God
has set before us.*

Hebrews 12:1 NLT

Dear Heavenly Father,

On days like today, my responsibilities seem to over-whelm me. I'm running as fast as I can, but I don't seem to be making progress. My feet feel like they could fly out from under me at any moment.

Lord, give me that boost of energy and determination I need to get me around this turn and onto the back-stretch. Help me focus my eyes on You until the finish line is in sight. Be the wind that propels me forward even when I lose confidence in my own strength and fortitude. Keep me on my feet until I finish the race and hear You say, "Well done."

Amen.

*Patient endurance is what you need now, so you will continue to do
God's will. Then you will receive all that he has promised.*

Hebrews 10:36 NLT

MY PERSONAL PRAYER

*By perseverance
the snail reached the ark.*
Charles Haddon Spurgeon

Dear Father:

———————————————————————

———————————————————————

———————————————————————

———————————————————————

———————————————————————

———————————————————————

———————————————————————

Amen

*Endurance develops strength of character in us, and character
strengthens our confident expectation of salvation.*
Romans 5:4 NLT

*I'm staying on your trail; I'm putting one foot in front of the
other. I'm not giving up.*
Psalm 17:5 MSG

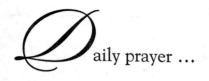 aily prayer ...

for purpose

> *We are God's masterpiece. He has created us*
> *anew in Christ Jesus, so that we can do the*
> *good things he planned for us long ago.*
>
> Ephesians 2:10 NLT

Dear Heavenly Father,

I cherish the roles I occupy in the lives of those around me—wife, mother, daughter, and friend. I see them all as positions of honor and privilege, and I recognize that You are the one who placed me in these roles. And yet, I cannot define myself by any one of them, for they are always changing and evolving.

Ultimately, my purpose for being alive can be revealed only by You, the one who created me. You are the one who placed within me a unique combination of talents and personality traits and strengths and insights and passions. Open my eyes, Lord, to see myself in light of Your eternal purpose.

Amen.

> *The LORD will fulfill his purpose for me;*
> *your love, O LORD, endures forever.*
>
> Psalm 138:8 NIV

MY PERSONAL PRAYER

The only possible answer to the destiny of man is to seek without respite to fulfill God's purpose.
Paul Tournier

Dear Father:

_____

_____

_____

_____

_____

_____

Amen

My life is God's prayer.
Psalm 42:8 MSG

People can make many different plans.
But only the Lord's plan will happen.
Proverbs 19:21 NCV

*D*aily prayer ...

for my spouse

*Above all things have fervent love
for one another, for "love will cover
a multitude of sins."*

1 Peter 4:8 NKJV

Dear Heavenly Father,

When I got married, I had an image in my mind—an image of the perfect man, my knight in shining armor, my romantic, witty, charming crusader for everything right and just. Apparently, I forgot that I was marrying a human being, a mere mortal like myself.

Now, Lord, the clouds in my head have parted. I see the wonderful man that he is, trying so hard to love and care for me in a way that's pleasing to You—a man who often gets it right and sometimes gets it wrong. Bless him with confidence, courage, and clear-headedness as he faithfully meets his often-overwhelming responsibilities. Cover him with Your hand and sustain him with Your love.

Amen.

Wives submit to your own husbands, as is fitting in the Lord.
Colossians 3:18 NKJV

MY PERSONAL PRAYER

*Successful marriage is always
a triangle: a man, a woman,
and God.*

Cecil Myers

Dear Father:

_____

_____

_____

_____

_____

_____

Amen

Remain faithful to one another in marriage.
Hebrews 13:4 NLT

*Find a good spouse, you find a good life—
and even more: the favor of GOD!*
Proverbs 18:22 MSG

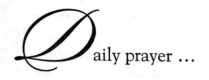

Daily prayer ...

for my children

Children are a gift from God: they are his reward.

Psalm 127:3 TLB

Dear Heavenly Father,

You know my children better than I ever will—and love them more than I ever could. As a mom, I so often feel as though my children's lives are in my hands, as though their safety and their future rest on how good of a mother I turn out to be.

But, my children's lives are in Your hands, not mine. I will never be the perfect parent to them. Only You can fill that role. Draw them close to You today, with the gentle care of a loving Father, Creator, and Friend. Be their solid rock of hope and protection every day of their lives.

Amen.

*Teach your children to choose the right path,
and when they are older, they will remain upon it.*
Proverbs 22:6 NLT

MY PERSONAL PRAYER

We can't form our children on our own concepts; we must take them and love them as God gives them to us.

Johann Wolfgang von Goethe

Dear Father:

_____

_____

_____

_____

_____

_____

_____

Amen

For this child I prayed, and the LORD has granted me my petition which I asked of Him.
1 Samuel 1:27 NKJV

Commit everything you do to the Lord. Trust him to help you do it and he will.
Psalm 37:5 TLB

Prayers to Encourage and Comfort the Soul

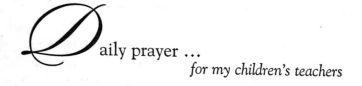

*D*aily prayer ...
for my children's teachers

A wise teacher makes learning a joy.
Proverbs 15:2 TLB

Dear Heavenly Father,

Guide my children's teachers. Even if they don't believe in You, work behind the scenes to soften their hearts toward You and toward the students You've entrusted into their care.

Give them eyes to see every one of their students as precious, a true miracle in progress. Give them patience for each and every day in the classroom. Bless them with wisdom, compassion, and honest words of encouragement that will help make a positive difference in these children's lives—including the lives of my own kids.

Thank You, Lord, for these teachers and the important task You have assigned them to. Help us never to take them for granted.

Amen.

The teaching of the wise is a fountain of life.
Proverbs 13:14 MSG

MY PERSONAL PRAYER

*I thank them that pray for me
when my bell tolls.*

John Donne

Dear Father:

_____

_____

_____

_____

_____

_____

Amen

Knowledge flows like spring water from the wise.
Proverbs 15:2 MSG

Take all the help you can get; every weapon God has issued.
Ephesians 6:13 MSG

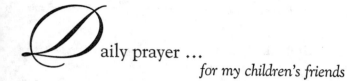

*D*aily prayer …

for my children's friends

The earnest prayer of a righteous person has
great power and wonderful results.

James 5:16 NLT

Dear Heavenly Father,

I pray for those young people who have developed
friendships with my children. Increase my love for each
one of them in a visible and genuine way. Let our home
be a haven of peace and righteousness for them, a blessing every time they enter.

You know each of these precious ones by name—and
by heart. Make me sensitive to their needs, wise concerning their weaknesses, and affirming in regard to
their strengths. Help me diligently watch for signs of
trouble and steer them away from danger as I would my
own children.

Lord, help me remember that our love and acceptance
may be the only witness of Your love that these young
people will ever know.

Amen.

Jesus said, "By this all will know that you are My disciples,
if you have love for one another."

John 13:35 NKJV

MY PERSONAL PRAYER

*Insomuch as any one
pushes you nearer to God,
he or she is your friend.*
Author Unknown

Dear Father:

_____

_____

_____

_____

_____

_____

Amen

A sweet friendship refreshes the soul.
Proverbs 27:9 MSG

Friends love through all kinds of weather.
Proverbs 17:17 MSG

aily prayer ...

for my siblings

*Jesus said, "Whoever does the will of God is
My brother and My sister and mother."*

Mark 3:34 NKJV

Dear Heavenly Father,

I love being part of Your family. I love having a Father in heaven who delights in me, quirks and all. And I love having spiritual brothers and sisters, people with whom I can share my faith in God and my priorities in life.

It's different with some of my natural siblings. I can't imagine how we could have less in common. And yet, I believe that You put us in the same family for a reason. Even when that reason isn't apparent, increase my love for each one as a way of honoring my earthly parents and my heavenly Father. And I pray that You will draw us closer together in that love.

Amen.

*A believer should take care of his own relatives, especially his own family.
If he does not do that, he has turned against the faith.*

1 Timothy 5:8 NCV

MY PERSONAL PRAYER

If we truly love people, we will desire for them far more than it is within our power to give them, and this will lead us to prayer. Intercession is a way of loving others.

Richard Foster

Dear Father:

_____

_____

_____

_____

_____

_____

Amen

God places the lonely in families.
Psalm 68:6 NLT

Pray every way you know how, for everyone you know.
1 Timothy 2:1 MSG

Prayers to Encourage and Comfort the Soul   53

Daily prayer …

for my parents

Listen with respect to the father who raised you; and when your mother grows old, don't neglect her.

Proverbs 23:22 MSG

Dear Heavenly Father,

I'm no longer a toddler or a teen. I'm an adult. Yet, I'll always be my parents' daughter, no matter what my age. I need Your help in relating to my parents as more than just fellow adults. I want to treat them in a way that makes You smile—with love, respect, and grace.

But, I find that it's a tricky business balancing the needs of my parents with the needs of my family—not to mention my own needs. Sometimes I feel like I'm failing everyone. Show me each day how to handle things in the very best way possible. Give me insight into what to do and say, and even how to pray for the people I love.

Amen.

This is the promise: If you honor your father and other, "you will live a long life, full of blessing."
Ephesians 6:2, 3 NLT

MY PERSONAL PRAYER

*When you have children,
you begin to understand
what you owe your parents.*
Japanese Proverb

Dear Father:

_____

_____

_____

_____

_____

_____

Amen

If you love wisdom, you'll delight your parents.
Proverbs 29:3 MSG

*Show respect to the aged, honor the presence of an elder,
fear your God.*
Leviticus 19:32 MSG

Prayers to Encourage and Comfort the Soul 55

Daily prayer ...

for my friends

*Just as water reflects the face, so one human
heart reflects another.*

Proverbs 27:19 NRSV

Dear Heavenly Father,

There are no words to express my gratitude for the circle
of friends You've given me. Each one is different, like a
rare gemstone fashioned to best reflect Your light in a
uniquely beautiful way. Thank You for both the smiles
and tears we've shared and for the wonderful moments
of friendship that are yet to come.

Lord, I also pray that You will help me to be honest
with my friends and open to the truth when they are
honest with me. Teach me to appreciate confrontation
born of love and give You thanks for friends who don't
run away from uncomfortable situations. Bless them for
all the wonderful things they bring to my life.

Amen.

I always pray for you, and I make my requests with a heart full of joy.
Philippians 1:3 NLT

MY PERSONAL PRAYER

*A true friend is a gift of God,
and he only who made hearts
can unite them.*

Robert South

Dear Father:

_____

_____

_____

_____

_____

_____

_____

Amen

Be devoted to one another in brotherly love.
Romans 12:10 NIV

*Friends come and friends go,
but a true friend sticks by you like family.*
Proverbs 18:24 MSG

Prayers to Encourage and Comfort the Soul

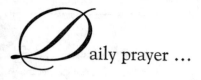aily prayer ...

for my neighbors

> *Don't talk about your neighbors behind their backs—no slander or gossip, please.*
> Proverbs 24:28 MSG

Dear Heavenly Father,

My neighborhood is more than a place; it's also a group of people. Some are young; others old. Some are pleasant and thoughtful; others are difficult. Some are friendly and outgoing; others want to be left alone.

I pray for each one, Lord—for those who are easy to love and those who are not. Give me wisdom and insight into their needs and compassion and patience with their eccentricities. Give me opportunities to speak words of encouragement, while avoiding hypocrisy, pat answers, gossip, and self-righteous advice.

I want to be a neighbor who can be depended on. One who is pleasing in Your sight. One who is willing to put aside petty annoyances and differences that peace may reign.

Amen

It is better to go to a neighbor than to a relative who lives far away.
Proverbs 27:10 NLT

MY PERSONAL PRAYER

I am to become a Christ to my neighbor and be for him what Christ is for me.

Martin Luther

Dear Father:

_____

_____

_____

_____

_____

_____

_____

Amen

Jesus said, "Love your neighbor as you love yourself."
Matthew 19:19 NCV

Let your light shine before men, that they may see your good deeds and praise your Father in heaven.
Matthew 5:16 NIV

*D*aily prayer ...

for my enemies

Jesus said, "Love your enemies. Pray for those who hurt you."

Matthew 5:44 NCV

Dear Heavenly Father,

I know You didn't design my heart to hate. You created my heart in the very image of Your own. You created it for love. But, there are people You've brought into my life who I wish I'd never met. People who rub me the wrong way or get on my nerves. There are even those who I wish You would punish for the way they've treated me.

Lord, when I'm tempted to wallow in resentment, help me remember how badly I've treated You—and yet, You have chosen to forgive me. Then, help me extend that same grace and forgiveness toward my enemies, regardless of whether they choose to accept my forgiveness or not.

Amen.

Christ suffered, but he did not threaten. He let God, the One who judges rightly, take care of him.
1 Peter 2:23 NCV

MY PERSONAL PRAYER

You never so touch the ocean of God's love as when you forgive and love your enemies.

Corrie ten Boom

Dear Father:

_____

_____

_____

_____

_____

_____

_____

Amen

Do not rejoice when your enemies fall into trouble.
Don't be happy when they stumble.
Proverbs 24:17 NLT

When we please the LORD,
even our enemies make friends with us.
Proverbs 16:7 CEV

Prayers to Encourage and Comfort the Soul 61

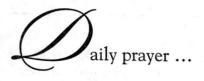

Daily prayer ...

for my community

Don't desecrate the land in which you live. I live here too—I, GOD, live in the same neighborhood.

Numbers 35:34 MSG

Dear Heavenly Father,

Beyond my neighborhood is a community that needs You. I'm just one woman, but I believe that one woman who's willing to be used by You can make a positive change in her surroundings. Show me how—whether it's through the power of prayer, getting involved socially or politically, or simply being a good citizen and compassionate neighbor.

Give our community leaders wisdom that is beyond their own understanding. Help them transform this neighborhood into one that better reflects Your values.

Lord, I believe You placed me here for a reason. Help me to be a positive force for good right here in my own corner of the world.

Amen.

Clean living before God and justice with our neighbors mean far more to GOD than religious performance.

Proverbs 21:3 MSG

MY PERSONAL PRAYER

*Community is the place where God
completes our lives with his joy.*
Henri Nouwen

Dear Father:

_____

_____

_____

_____

_____

_____

Amen

Unless the Lord protects a city, sentries do no good.
Psalm 127:1 TLB

When right–living people bless the city, it flourishes.
Proverbs 11:11 MSG

 aily prayer ...

for those in need

*Mercy to the needy is a loan to GOD, and
GOD pays back those loans in full.*

Proverbs 19:17 MSG

Dear Heavenly Father,

You've been so generous to me. Trying to count my
blessings would be as futile as trying to count the stars
in Your sky. As You continue to open my eyes to Your
graciousness to me, make me more aware of the needs
of those around me, particularly those You would like
me to help in a practical way.

Push me to move beyond just giving when it's easy.
Whether it's spiritually, physically, or financially, teach
me how to meet the needs of others by giving of my
time, energy, and resources without being pretentious
or condescending. Give me a cheerful heart, Lord, with
which to serve You and my fellowman.

Amen.

*Learn to do good, to be fair and to help the poor,
the fatherless, and widows.*

Isaiah 1:17 TLB

MY PERSONAL PRAYER

*When we serve the poor and
the sick, we serve Jesus.*
Rose of Lima

Dear Father:

_____

_____

_____

_____

_____

_____

Amen

*Generous hands are blessed hands
because they give bread to the poor.*
Proverbs 22:9 MSG

*Don't get tired of helping others. You will be rewarded when
the time is right, if you don't give up.*
Galatians 6:9 CEV

Prayers to Encourage and Comfort the Soul

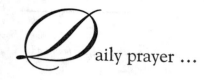

Daily prayer ...

for my country

Blessed is the nation whose God is the Lord.
Psalm 33:12 TLB

Dear Heavenly Father,

I realize that the freedoms I enjoy came at a terrible price. I will always be grateful to those courageous individuals who suffered and died for the cause of freedom. I pray for those who are even now fighting for liberty and justice.

Strengthen our president. Give him the courage to stand up for what is right, even in the face of criticism. And I ask that You place Your hand of protection over his life and the lives of his loved ones.

Lord, I pray also for the judges who make critical decisions for the good of others, and the legislators who have committed their time and talents to creating and maintaining our laws. May wisdom and knowledge reign in their midst.

Amen.

Be a good citizen. All governments are under God.
Insofar as there is peace and order, it's God's order.
Romans 13:1 MSG

MY PERSONAL PRAYER

*We must make of our country
not an idol, but a stepping-stone
toward God.*

Simone Weil

Dear Father:

_____

_____

_____

_____

_____

_____

Amen

We are citizens of heaven.
Philippians 3:20 NLT

*All kings shall fall down before Him;
all nations shall serve Him.*
Psalm 72:11 NKJV

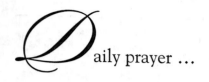aily prayer ...

for the world

> *Be still, and know that I am God; I will be exalted among the nations, I will be exalted in the earth!*
>
> Psalm 46:10 NKJV

Dear Heavenly Father,

I feel like such a small dot of humanity on Your enormous earth. Help me see beyond my little corner of the world. Remind me to pray for people and places all around the globe, including those I wouldn't even be able to locate on a map.

Encourage men and women who are working beyond our borders to spread the good news of Your love. Remind me to pray regularly for them and support them with my financial gifts, for it is in large part through their efforts that the world will be ready for Your coming.

Amen.

Jesus told his disciples, "Go and make disciples of all the nations, baptizing them in the name of the Father and the Son and the Holy Spirit."
Matthew 28:19 NLT

MY PERSONAL PRAYER   *God shapes the world by prayer.*
                                       E. M. Bounds

Dear Father:

_____

_____

_____

_____

_____

_____

                                              Amen

The earth is filled with his tender love.
Psalm 33:5 TLB

Peoples from the remotest lands will worship him.
Psalm 67:7 TLB

Prayers to Encourage and Comfort the Soul   69

The Helper

The little sharp vexations,
And the briars, that catch and fret,
Why not take all to The Helper
Who has never failed us yet?
Tell Him about the heartache,
And tell Him the longings too;
Tell Him the baffled purpose
When we scarce know what to do;
Then leaving all our weakness
With the One divinely strong;
Forget that we bore the burden,
And carry away the song.

Phillips Brooks

Daily Prayers for Help ...

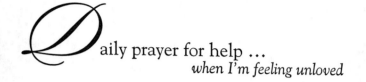

Daily prayer for help ...
when I'm feeling unloved

I'll call nobodies and make them somebodies;
I'll call the unloved and make them beloved.

Romans 9:25 MSG

Dear Heavenly Father,

I feel like a hole has opened in my heart and all the love has seeped right out. I am keenly aware of my insignificance and wonder if I am even worthy of love. I would lose hope and despair if I did not know the truth—Your love for me is unconditional and everlasting.

Unlike the love of those around me, even those closest to me, Your love will never fail. It began before I was born and will last throughout eternity.

I need to feel a touch of Your faithful love right now, Lord. Soothe my aching heart with the truth that I am so dear to You that You would even ask Your precious Son, Jesus, to die for me.

Amen.

God is so rich in mercy, and he loved us so very much,
that even while we were dead because of our sins,
he gave us life when he raised Christ from the dead.

Ephesians 2:4 NLT

MY PERSONAL PRAYER

All God can give us is his love; and this love becomes tangible—a burning of the soul—it sets us on fire to the point of forgetting ourselves.

Brother Roger

Dear Father:

_____

_____

_____

_____

_____

_____

Amen

What marvelous love the father has extended to us! Just look at it—we're called children of God! That's who we really are.
1 John 3:1 MSG

Your unfailing love, O LORD, is as vast as the heavens; your faithfulness reaches beyond the clouds.
Psalm 36:5 NLT

Prayers to Encourage and Comfort the Soul

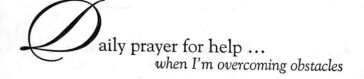

Daily prayer for help …
when I'm overcoming obstacles

Listen closely to my prayer, O LORD; hear
my urgent cry. I will call to you whenever
trouble strikes, and you will answer me.

Psalm 86:6, 7 NLT

Dear Heavenly Father,

My life is so difficult right now. I just get clear of one
giant obstacle—bills, illness, people problems—and two
more pop up in my path. I know I will never overcome
them all without Your help.

No matter what lies ahead, I want to rely on You for
guidance and perseverance. When I start to fall back
on my own strength and try to work things out my way
instead of Yours, stop me. I don't want to move ahead
until I'm sure my steps are secure and ordered by You.
Then, with Your help, I know I can overcome anything
that comes my way.

Amen.

You know all about it—the contempt, the abuse. I dare to believe that
the luckless will get lucky someday in you. You won't let them down.
Psalm 10:14 MSG

MY PERSONAL PRAYER

Any concern too small to be turned into a prayer is too small to be made into a burden.

Corrie ten Boom

Dear Father:

_____

_____

_____

_____

_____

_____

Amen

Is anything too hard for the LORD?
Genesis 18:14 NKJV

If one of you is having troubles, he should pray.
James 5:13 NCV

Prayers to Encourage and Comfort the Soul　　75

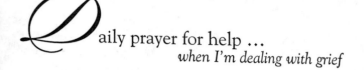

Daily prayer for help ...
when I'm dealing with grief

Your sun shall never set; the moon shall not go down—for the Lord will be your everlasting light; your days of mourning all will end.

Isaiah 60:20 TLB

Dear Heavenly Father,

If anyone knows how it feels to have a broken heart, Lord, it's You. You watched Your own Son die a terrible death on the cross. You've watched those You love suffer in the grip of evil. You have experienced grief firsthand.

My heart is broken, Lord. It seems like the ache will never go away. Only Your touch—the touch of one who has felt what I feel, who has lost as much as I have lost—can comfort me now. Only You can restore my hope, my peace, my ability to love. Only You can help me keep on living. Please wrap Your presence around me like a warm blanket on a stormy night.

Amen.

The Lamb on the Throne will shepherd them, will lead them to spring waters of Life. And God will wipe every last tear from their eyes.
Revelations 7:17 MSG

MY PERSONAL PRAYER

*If they are with Christ
and Christ is with us,
then they cannot be very far away.*
Pierre Teilhard de Chardin

Dear Father:

_____

_____

_____

_____

_____

_____

_____

Amen

*Jesus said, "God blesses those who mourn,
for they will be comforted."*
Matthew 5:4 NLT

*The LORD is close to the brokenhearted;
he rescues those who are crushed in spirit.*
Psalm 34:18 NLT

Prayers to Encourage and Comfort the Soul

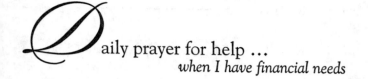

Daily prayer for help ...
when I have financial needs

*Your heavenly Father already knows your
needs, and he will give you all you need from
day to day if you live for him and make the
Kingdom of God your primary concern.*

Matthew 6:32, 33 NLT

Dear Heavenly Father,

Jesus told us to pray for our "daily bread." I need more
than just bread today, Lord. I need Your wisdom, as
well as Your provision. I need to know how to plug the
holes in my financial bucket. I need to know ways to
increase my income and balance my budget.

I know You're aware of my every need. You know the
balance in my checkbook and the amount of every bill I
need to pay. Show me how to do my part and then let
You do Yours. Even now, I thank You for seeing us
through this current crisis—for giving us our daily bread.

Amen.

*My God will use his wonderful riches in Christ Jesus
to give you everything you need.*
Philippians 4:19 NCV

MY PERSONAL PRAYER

*Pray as though everything
depended on God. Work as though
everything depended on you.*
Saint Augustine

Dear Father:

_____

_____

_____

_____

_____

_____

Amen

The Lord's blessing is our greatest wealth.
Proverbs 10:22 TLB

*Those of us who reverence the Lord
will never lack any good thing.*
Psalm 34:10 TLB

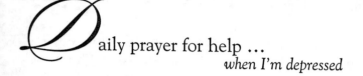

Daily prayer for help …
when I'm depressed

When I was in deep trouble, I searched for the Lord. All night long I pray, with hands lifted toward heaven, pleading. There can be no joy for me until he acts.

Psalm 77:2 NLT

Dear Heavenly Father,

You came up with the design for women, both inside and out. You know how circumstances, relational situations, and even hormones play a part in my emotions and overall feelings about life. Right now, my emotions have bottomed out. I've lost sight of joy and hope.

Please speak clearly to the deepest part of me. Encourage me in a way that goes deeper than the words of friends or even the love of a spouse. Lift me out of this depression, whether circumstances change or not. When my emotions push me toward believing something that is not in line with Your truth, give me the strength to trust what You say more than what I feel. Restore my joy for living, I pray.

Amen.

God's a safe house for the battered, a sanctuary during bad times. The moment you arrive, you relax; you're never sorry you knocked.

Psalm 9:9, 10 MSG

MY PERSONAL PRAYER

When you come to the bottom,
you find God.

Neville Talbot

Dear Father:

_____

_____

_____

_____

_____

_____

Amen

If God cares so wonderfully for flowers that are here today
and gone tomorrow, won't he more surely care for you?
Matthew 6:30 NLT

You keep track of all my sorrows. You have collected all my
tears in your bottle. You have recorded each one in your book.
Psalm 56:8 NLT

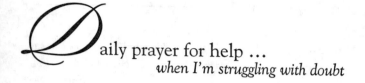

aily prayer for help ...
when I'm struggling with doubt

*Lord, when doubts fill my mind, when my
heart is in turmoil, quiet me and give me
renewed hope and cheer.*

Psalm 94:19 TLB

Dear Heavenly Father,

I don't ask to understand You completely—no one could
do that. I realize that Your ways, Your thoughts are high
above my own. What I do ask is to find resolution for
the doubts and uncertainties that cloud my mind and
keep me from fully embracing my faith in You.

I believe You are great enough to be patient with my
silly, wandering mind, Lord. When my doubting heart
threatens to forsake me, second guess me, derail my
resolve to follow You, quiet me with Your presence, and
open my heart to hear Your voice bearing gifts of assurance and understanding.

Amen.

*Trust in the LORD with all your heart, and lean not on your own
understanding. In all your ways acknowledge Him and
He shall direct your paths.*

Proverbs 3:5, 6 NKJV

MY PERSONAL PRAYER

*Doubts are the ants in the pants
of faith. They keep it awake
and moving.*

Frederick Buechner

Dear Father:

_____

_____

_____

_____

_____

_____

Amen

Show mercy to those whose faith is wavering.
Jude 22 NLT

*The word of the LORD holds true,
and everything he does is worthy of our trust.*
Psalm 33:4 NLT

Prayers to Encourage and Comfort the Soul

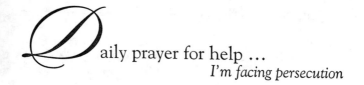

Daily prayer for help …
I'm facing persecution

*If people persecute you because you are a
Christian, don't curse them; pray that
God will bless them.*

Romans 12:14 NLT

Dear Heavenly Father,

You know how much I want others to like me, to make
me feel as though I belong. Help me remember that
first and foremost I belong to You. Make me bold
enough to say what needs to be said about You, wise
enough to know when to speak and when to remain
silent, and loving enough to not just talk, but listen.
When words won't work, show me how to put Your
love into action, preaching a sermon in silence.

Give me the grace to endure whatever comes my way as
a result of my faith in You. Help me to bear it faithfully,
without complaint, as an expression of my love for You.

Amen.

*Count yourselves blessed every time people put you down
or throw you out or speak lies about you to discredit me.
What it means is that the truth is too close for comfort.*

Matthew 5:11 MSG

MY PERSONAL PRAYER

Jesus promised his disciples three things—that they would be completely fearless, absurdly happy and in constant trouble.

G.K. Chesterton

Dear Father:

_____

_____

_____

_____

_____

_____

Amen

I come to you for protection, O LORD my God.
Save me from my persecutors—rescue me!
Psalm 7:1 NLT

Jesus said, "Since they persecuted me,
naturally they will persecute you."
John 15:20 NLT

Prayers to Encourage and Comfort the Soul

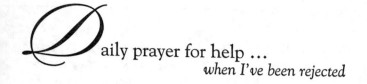

Daily prayer for help ...
when I've been rejected

Your love has always been our lives' foundation,
your fidelity has been the roof over our world.
Psalm 89:2 MSG

Dear Heavenly Father,

Your Son endured a great deal of rejection. A friend boldly betrayed him. Another close friend denied even knowing Him. I don't understand how He could continue to love and forgive them. I want to be more like Him. But when I try on my own, I can't do it.

Being rejected just makes me angry and confused. I feel myself wanting to fight back, to prove that I am a woman of worth. I do realize that I can't control what others say and do. I can't control what they think about me. All I can do is live my life with integrity and rest in the fact that You know the truth about me.

Amen.

He was despised and rejected—a man of sorrows,
acquainted with bitterest grief.
Isaiah 53:3 NLT

MY PERSONAL PRAYER

Rejection is the sand in the oyster,
the irritant that ultimately produces
the pearl.

Burke Wilkinson

Dear Father:

_____

_____

_____

_____

_____

_____

Amen

Even if my father and mother abandon me,
the LORD will hold me close.
Psalm 27:10 NLT

Overlook an offense and bond a friendship;
fasten on to a slight and—goodbye, friend!
Proverbs 17:9 MSG

Prayers to Encourage and Comfort the Soul   87

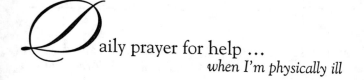

Daily prayer for help …
when I'm physically ill

*The way God designed our bodies is a model
for understanding our lives together as a
church … If one part hurts, every other part
is involved in the hurt, and in the healing.*
1 Corinthians 12:25, 26 MSG

Dear Heavenly Father,

My body is aching. I've done everything I know to
do—sought the help of a doctor, faithfully followed his
instructions, availed myself of the proper medications—
and still, my body is in distress. I need Your help, Lord.
I need the hand that created me to reach down and
restore me.

I believe it is Your will for me to be whole and healthy
in every way—physically, emotionally, and spiritually. I
ask You for that now. I move my focus from my present
distress to Your unfailing love. Thank You for hearing
me and doing for me what I cannot do for myself.

Amen.

God nurses them when they are sick, and soothes their pains and worries.
Psalm 41:3 TLB

MY PERSONAL PRAYER

*There is nothing the body suffers
that the soul may not profit by.*
George Meredith

Dear Father:

_____

_____

_____

_____

_____

_____

_____

Amen

God is my helper. The Lord is the one who keeps me alive!
Psalm 54:4 NLT

*Are any among you sick? They should call for the elders of
the church and have them pray over them.*
James 5:14 NLT

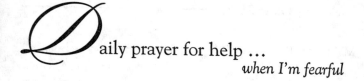

*D*aily prayer for help ...
when I'm fearful

> *Don't panic. I'm with you. There's no need*
> *to fear for I'm your God. I'll give you*
> *strength. I'll help you. I'll hold you steady,*
> *keep a firm grip on you.*
>
> Isaiah 41:10 MSG

Dear Heavenly Father,

I can't seem to calm my anxious heart. But, I know You
can. Even if the circumstances that surround me
remain the same, You can help me find a place of peace
when I'm facing what I fear the most.

You are bigger than everything I fear. You also know
the real reasons behind why I'm afraid, what's hidden
in my heart from even me. You know where the seed of
my anxiety lies. Open my eyes to better understand the
lies that lay at the root of my fears. Quiet my anxious
heart and thoughts with the balm of Your truth.

Amen.

The very hairs on your head are all numbered. So don't be afraid.
Matthew 10:30, 31 NLT

MY PERSONAL PRAYER

There is never a fear that has not a corresponding "Fear not."
Amy Carmichael

Dear Father:

_____

_____

_____

_____

_____

_____

Amen

We can say with confidence, "The Lord is my helper, so I will not be afraid. What can mere mortals do to me?"
Hebrews 13:6 NLT

God ordered his angels to guard you wherever you go.
Psalm 91:11 MSG

Prayers to Encourage and Comfort the Soul

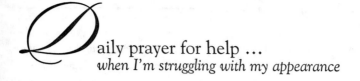

Daily prayer for help ...
when I'm struggling with my appearance

We are God's masterpiece.
Ephesians 2:10 NLT

Dear Heavenly Father,

I don't like what I see in the mirror today. But, Lord, I know that when You look at me You always see something of beauty. It doesn't matter what size dress I wear, whether I'm having a good hair day or a bad hair day, if I stand out in a crowd or if I take my place among the wallflowers. You call me beautiful. You call me precious. You call me Yours.

Help me break my habit of comparing myself with others. When I look in the mirror, I want to see myself the way You see me—a unique creation of almighty God.

Amen.

Cultivate inner beauty, the gentle gracious kind that God delights in.
1 Peter 3:4 MSG

MY PERSONAL PRAYER

God's fingers can touch nothing but to mold it into loveliness.
George MacDonald

Dear Father:

_____

_____

_____

_____

_____

_____

_____

Amen

People judge by outward appearance, but the LORD looks at a person's thoughts and intentions.
1 Samuel 16:7 NLT

God has made everything beautiful in its time.
Ecclesiastes 3:11 NKJV

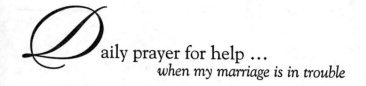

Daily prayer for help ...
when my marriage is in trouble

*Marriage is not a place to "stand up for
your rights." Marriage is a decision to serve
the other.*

1 Corinthians 7:4 MSG

Dear Heavenly Father,

I know marriage is a lifelong commitment in Your eyes.
I also know that I'm an imperfect woman who's married
to an imperfect man. Only with Your help will we be
able to continue to love, forgive, and communicate
with each other.

Help me see any weaknesses in my character that are
causing trouble in our relationship. Deal with any pride,
selfishness, anger, or bitterness I may be holding onto.
Work in my husband's life too, I pray. Heal any hurts he
has suffered at my hands. Help him to realize that our
marriage is a gift from You—a gift worth holding onto.

Amen.

*Be kind to each other, tenderhearted, forgiving one another,
just as God through Christ has forgiven you.*
Ephesians 4:32 NLT

MY PERSONAL PRAYER

Marriages are made in heaven.
Alfred Lord Tennyson

Dear Father:

_____

_____

_____

_____

_____

_____

_____

Amen

*Every one of us needs to pray; when all hell breaks loose and
the dam bursts we'll be on high ground, untouched.*
Psalm 32:6 MSG

Have respect for marriage.
Hebrews 13:4 CEV

Prayers to Encourage and Comfort the Soul

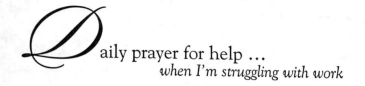

Daily prayer for help …
when I'm struggling with work

> *Put GOD in charge of your work, then what*
> *you've planned will take place.*
>
> Proverbs 16:3 MSG

Dear Heavenly Father,

Whatever I do, I want to do it in a way that pleases You. Help me be faithful in doing my best with every task that's set before me, regardless of how rewarding, stressful, tedious, or impossible it feels at the moment. I need Your strength to help me persevere when I'd rather procrastinate, Your words of encouragement to lift my spirits when my diligence goes unnoticed or unappreciated.

Whether I'm at work inside my own home or in the marketplace, keep me conscious of Your presence. Everywhere is the right place to talk to You.

Amen.

It is not that we think we can do anything of lasting value by ourselves.
Our only power and success come from God.
2 Corinthians 3:5 NLT

MY PERSONAL PRAYER

Pray, then and work.
Work and pray. And still
again pray, and then work.
George Müller

Dear Father:

_____

_____

_____

_____

_____

_____

Amen

Stay calm; mind your own business; do your own job.
1 Thessalonians 4:11 MSG

GOD cares about honesty in the workplace;
your business is his business.
Proverbs 16:11 MSG

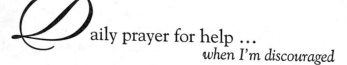

Daily prayer for help …
when I'm discouraged

I want you woven into a tapestry of love, in touch with everything there is to know of God. Then you will have minds confident and at rest, focused on Christ, God's great mystery.

Colossians 2:2 MSG

Dear Heavenly Father,

Life just isn't going the way I thought it would. Sometimes, I feel like it's no use dreaming about "good things" that may be waiting for me around the corner, because I just keep getting hit with disappointment. I know this is not the life, or at least the attitude, that You want for me.

Give me a glimmer of hope, a glimpse of Your big picture. Strengthen me with words of encouragement. Whether they come through time spent with You and Your Word or through the loving support of my family and friends, open my ears so I don't miss them. Let me cling to them like a drowning woman clings to a lifeboat, trusting You to keep my head above water.

Amen.

I'm eager to encourage you in your faith, but I also want to be encouraged by yours. In this way, each of us will be a blessing to the other.
Romans 1:12 NLT

MY PERSONAL PRAYER

When we yield to discouragement, it is usually because we give too much thought to the past or the future.
Saint Thérèse of Lisieux

Dear Father:

_____

_____

_____

_____

_____

_____

Amen

Don't be afraid or discouraged by the size of the task, for the LORD God, my God, is with you. He will not fail you or forsake you.
1 Chronicles 28:20 NLT

God, who encourages those who are discouraged, encouraged us.
2 Corinthians 7:6 NLT

Prayers to Encourage and Comfort the Soul

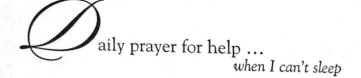

Daily prayer for help …
when I can't sleep

*If I'm sleepless at midnight, I spend the hours
in grateful reflection.*

Psalm 63:6 MSG

Dear Heavenly Father,

I feel like I'm wasting time and robbing myself of tomorrow's energy, but I just can't shut my mind down long enough to fall asleep. Help me turn every worry into a prayer. One by one, empty my mind of all of my plans and responsibilities—at least until morning comes.

Hold me in Your arms like a mother holds her newborn baby. Sing me a lullaby, every note filled with love and tenderness. Calm any anxious thoughts. Relax my restless body. Release every bit of tension in my neck and shoulders. Then, lead me into dreams that fill my heart with joy, refreshing me from the inside out for the day that lies ahead.

Amen.

It is useless to work so hard for a living, getting up early and going to bed late. For the LORD provides for those he loves, while they are asleep.

Psalm 127:2 GNT

MY PERSONAL PRAYER

Don't count sheep if you can't sleep. Talk to the shepherd.
Paul Frost

Dear Father:

_____

_____

_____

_____

_____

_____

Amen

I lie down and sleep; I wake again, for the LORD sustains me.
Psalm 3:5 NRSV

You can lie down without fear and enjoy pleasant dreams.
Proverbs 3:24 NLT

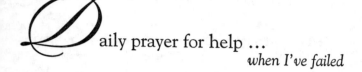

Daily prayer for help ...
when I've failed

Though I have fallen, I will rise. Though I sit
in darkness, the LORD will be my light.
Micah 7:8 NIV

Dear Heavenly Father,

My great expectations have disappeared into thin air. I feel like such a failure. Do You ever get tired of picking me up and brushing me off? Do You ever ask Yourself if I'm worth the effort?

Give me a fresh picture of the woman You created me to be, Lord—my abilities, my potential, my unique place in this world. Give me the courage to try again, even though I know I may not be finished with failing. Give me the ability to dream dreams again. Thank You for being the God of second chances ... and third chances ... and fourth chances ... and ....

Amen.

God's compassions never fail. They are new every morning.
Lamentations 3:22, 23 NIV

MY PERSONAL PRAYER

*Failure is God's own tool for
carving some of the finest outlines
in the character of his children.*
Thomas Hodgkin

Dear Father:

_____

_____

_____

_____

_____

_____

Amen

*You, O LORD, are a shield around me, my glory,
and the one who lifts up my head.*
Psalm 3:3 NRSV

Be strong and let your heart take courage.
Psalm 31:24 NRSV

Prayers to Encourage and Comfort the Soul   103

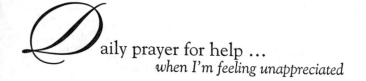

Daily prayer for help ...
when I'm feeling unappreciated

Our lives get in step with God and all others
by letting him set the pace, not by proudly or
anxiously trying to run the parade.

Romans 3:28 MSG

Dear Heavenly Father,

I know I'm supposed to be a servant, loving others unconditionally regardless of whether they are a member of my family or a stranger off the street. But, today I feel used. I feel like I serve others all the time and my efforts and hard work usually go unnoticed and unappreciated.

Still, Lord, I know that You see what I do both in public and in private. You know when I go the extra mile for someone. Help me to see when it's right to confront someone for taking advantage of me and when it's simply a matter of pride. I really do want to please You, Lord.

Amen.

Everyone I meet—it matters little whether they're mannered or rude,
smart or simple—deepens my sense of interdependence and obligation.

Romans 1:14 MSG

MY PERSONAL PRAYER

*Faithful service in a lowly place is
true spiritual greatness.*

D. Jackman

Dear Father:

_____

_____

_____

_____

_____

_____

Amen

*Serve wholeheartedly, as if you were
serving the Lord, not men.*
Ephesians 6:7 NIV

*If anyone serves, he should do it
with the strength God provides.*
1 Peter 4:11 NIV

Prayers to Encourage and Comfort the Soul

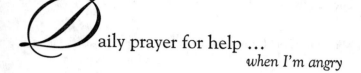

Daily prayer for help ...

when I'm angry

> *Let everyone be quick to listen, show to*
> *speak, slow to anger. For your anger does not*
> *produce God's righteousness.*
>
> James 1:19, 20 NRSV

Dear Heavenly Father,

My anger is simmering inside—and I feel justified in feeling this way. But, the strength of my emotions isn't a good barometer of the truth. I need You.

Clear my mind of angry emotions so I can begin to see this situation from Your perspective. Calm the tension in my body. Help me discern right from wrong, truth from lies. Help me subdue my pride long enough to take responsibility for any blame that may be mine.

Then, transform my anger into a positive plan for reconciliation. If I need to forgive or apologize, help me take steps in that direction. Replace my angry thoughts with gentle, healing words.

Amen.

A gentle response defuses anger, but a sharp tongue kindles a temper-fire.
Proverbs 15:1 MSG

MY PERSONAL PRAYER

As long as anger lives,
she continues to be the fruitful
mother of many unhappy children.
John Climacus

Dear Father:

_____

_____

_____

_____

_____

_____

Amen

Be angry but do not sin;
do not let the sun go down on your anger.
Ephesians 4:26 NRSV

One who is slow to anger is better than the mighty, and one
whose temper is controlled than one who captures a city.
Proverbs 16:32 NRSV

Prayers to Encourage and Comfort the Soul   107

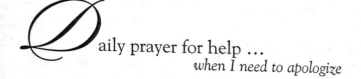

aily prayer for help ...
when I need to apologize

Confess your sins to each other and pray for each other so God can heal you.

James 5:16 NCV

Dear Heavenly Father,

I know I was wrong. Still ... it's hard to say "I'm sorry." Soften my heart so that I can give a sincere apology without any reservation. And give me the courage, the right timing, and the perfect words to say what needs to be said.

Stop me from bringing up any fault I see on the part of the other person. Let that remain between that person and You. If there needs to be time for healing, let me be patient. But, also let me be persistent in working toward reconciliation.

Lord, I know that when I hurt others, I also hurt You. So I begin my apology right here at Your feet. "I'm sorry, Lord."

Amen.

Jesus said, "First be reconciled to your brother or sister, and then come and offer your gift."

Matthew 5:24 NRSV

MY PERSONAL PRAYER

An apology is the superglue of life.
It can repair just about anything.
Lynn Johnston

Dear Father:

_____

_____

_____

_____

_____

_____

Amen

All of you should live together in peace.
1 Peter 3:8 NCV

Live in harmony with each other.
Romans 12:16 NLT

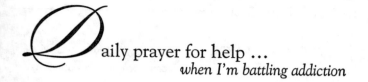

Daily prayer for help ...
when I'm battling addiction

> *The LORD your God is going before you.*
> *He will fight for you.*
>
> Deuteronomy 1:30 NLT

Dear Heavenly Father,

I want to be free from addition. I want to be healthy again for my own sake and especially for the people who love me and count on me. The trouble is—I'm afraid. What if I can't do it? What if I fail? I'm sure of this much; I can't do it on my own.

Open my eyes to see the truth where before I've believed lies. Open my heart to see the destruction my habit has caused in human terms. Open my understanding to see what it will be like on the other side of my addiction—a glimpse of freedom. I place myself in Your capable hands.

Amen.

> *You know that under pressure, your faith-life is forced*
> *into the open and shows its true colors.*
>
> James 1:3 MSG

MY PERSONAL PRAYER

Prayer is not conquering God's reluctance, but taking hold of God's willingness.

Phillips Brooks

Dear Father:

_____

_____

_____

_____

_____

_____

_____

Amen

Get down on your knees before the Master;
it's the only way you'll get on your feet.
James 4:10 MSG

Be strong in the Lord and in the strength of his power.
Ephesians 6:10 NRSV

My Dearest Lord

Be thou a bright flame before me,
Be thou a guiding star above me,
Be thou a smooth path beneath me,
Be thou a kindly shepherd behind me,
Today—tonight—and forever.

Saint Columba

Daily Prayers for Guidance …

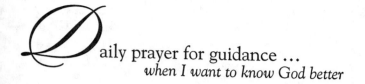

Daily prayer for guidance ...
when I want to know God better

I will give them a heart to know Me,
that I am the LORD.

Jeremiah 24:7 NKJV

Dear Heavenly Father,

I've always known that You love me. I've known that You died for me, and Your intentions toward me are good. But now, Lord, I feel a deep stirring inside to know You on a deeper level—to understand Your heart, to become familiar with Your character.

Really, I don't know how to say that in a formal way, except that I desire to know You better. Open my heart to receive more of You. Guide me as I read Your Word, that I might gain wisdom and insight into who You are. The Bible says to ask, so I'm asking. Show me something new about You every day.

Amen.

God wants us to grow up, to know the whole truth and tell it in love—
like Christ in everything.

Ephesians 4:15 MSG

MY PERSONAL PRAYER

To believe in God is one thing,
to know God another.

Staretz Silouan

Dear Father:

_____

_____

_____

_____

_____

_____

_____

Amen

Grow in the grace and knowledge of
our Lord and Savior Jesus Christ.
2 Peter 3:18 NIV

Jesus said, "This is the way to eternal life—to know you, the
only true God, and Jesus Christ, the one you sent to earth."
John 17:3 NLT

Prayers to Encourage and Comfort the Soul

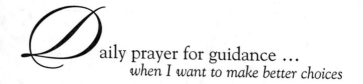

Daily prayer for guidance …
when I want to make better choices

> *The LORD says, "Stop right where you are!*
> *Look for the old, godly way, and walk in it.*
> *Travel its path, and you will find rest for*
> *your souls."*
>
> Jeremiah 6:16 NLT

Dear Heavenly Father,

I've made so many poor choices and suffered the consequences. I want to do the right thing from now on. Sure, I know I'll still mess up sometimes. But with Your help, I believe that I can do a better job of making good choices.

I know I will need Your strong hand to guide me. I don't expect You to make my decisions for me. I know that You've given me a free will. But right now, today, I submit my will to You. I promise to look to You before I act on emotion, before I take someone's word for something, before I make a choice by failing to make a choice. Thanks for guiding me in the way I should go.

Amen.

> *This is what the LORD Almighty says:*
> *"Give careful thought to your ways."*
> Haggai 1:5 NIV

MY PERSONAL PRAYER

*O Lord, may I be directed what to
do and what to leave undone.*
Elizabeth Fry

Dear Father:

_____

_____

_____

_____

_____

_____

Amen

*If any of you lacks wisdom, let him ask of God, who gives to
all liberally and without reproach, and it will be given to him.*
James 1:5 NKJV

*Grow a wise heart—you'll do yourself a favor;
keep a clear head—you'll find a good life.*
Proverbs 19:8 MSG

Prayers to Encourage and Comfort the Soul   117

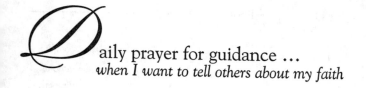

Daily prayer for guidance ...
when I want to tell others about my faith

*Faith comes from hearing the Good News,
and people hear the Good News when someone tells them about Christ.*

Romans 10:17 NCV

Dear Heavenly Father,

Knowing You has changed my life and given me the promise of spending eternity in heaven. I want others to know that they can also have the hope, the joy, and the help that is only a prayer away. But, I need courage, and the right words to speak.

I don't want to sound preachy or pushy. I want to share my own story, and Yours, with the love and conviction I honestly feel. Strengthen my resolve to share the Good News. Then, help me reach them to You. Help me to always remember that my faith shows through my actions as well as my words.

Amen.

*If you are asked about your Christian hope, always be ready to explain
it. But you must do this in a gentle and respectful way.*
1 Peter 3:15, 16 NLT

MY PERSONAL PRAYER

God is not saving the world; it is done. Our business is to get men and women to realize it.

Oswald Chambers

Dear Father:

_____

_____

_____

_____

_____

_____

Amen

Thank God! Pray to him by name!
Tell everyone you meet what he has done!
Psalm 105:1 MSG

I try to find common ground with everyone
so that I might bring them to Christ.
1 Corinthians 9:22 NLT

Prayers to Encourage and Comfort the Soul   119

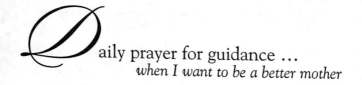

Daily prayer for guidance ...
when I want to be a better mother

> *Her children stand and bless her;*
> *so does her husband.*
>
> Proverbs 31:28 TLB

Dear Heavenly Father,

Thank You for my kids. Each one of them is a blessing and privilege, a beautiful and unique gift from You. Show me how to love them, Lord. Show me how to draw out their gifts and talents. I need Your guidance as I strive to teach my children how to love themselves and others, and, most of all, how to find Your will and purpose of their lives.

Being a mom can be so overwhelming at times—so many mistakes to make. I need Your help every moment of every day to be the mother my kids need, the mother You've designed me to be. Guide me, Lord.

Amen.

> *I have no greater joy than to hear*
> *that my children are walking in the truth.*
> 3 John 1:4 NIV

MY PERSONAL PRAYER

*The loveliest masterpiece
of the heart of God
is the heart of a mother.*
Thérèse of Lisieux

Dear Father:

_____

_____

_____

_____

_____

_____

Amen

*Train children in the right way, and when old,
they will not stray.*
Proverbs 22:6 NRSV

*All your children shall be taught by the Lord,
and great shall be the peace of your children.*
Isaiah 54:13 NKJV

Prayers to Encourage and Comfort the Soul

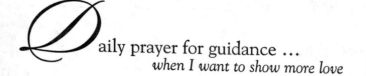

*D*aily prayer for guidance …
when I want to show more love

> *Most of all, love each other as if your life*
> *depended on it. Love makes up*
> *for practically anything.*
>
> 1 Peter 4:8 MSG

Dear Heavenly Father,

I deeply desire to love others in the way that pleases You. But I want to do more. My desire is to go beyond emotion and kind words and put my love into action, reaching out like You did to those who need it most.

Give me insight and empathy, energy and passion. Show me how to weep with those who weep and rejoice with those who rejoice—without expecting anything in return. I also ask for constancy, Lord. I want to be someone whose love can be counted on. Teach me to love like You love—selflessly, consistently, honestly, and unconditionally.

Amen.

> *The whole Law can be summed up in this one command.*
> *"Love others as you love yourself."*
>
> Galatians 5:14 TLB

MY PERSONAL PRAYER

Love lights more fires
than hate extinguishes.
Ella Wheeler Wilcox

Dear Father:

_____

_____

_____

_____

_____

_____

_____

Amen

Let us love one another, because love is of God.
1 John 4:7 NKJV

This is the message that you heard from the beginning,
that we should love one another.
1 John 3:11 NKJV

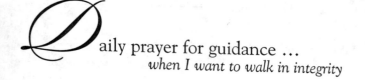

Daily prayer for guidance …
when I want to walk in integrity

*I know, my God, that you examine our
hearts and rejoice when you find
integrity there.*

1 Chronicles 29:17 NLT

Dear Heavenly Father,

Reveal to me any areas of my life that are not pleasing
to You—areas of dishonesty, mediocrity, or shady ethics.
I want to be a woman who is above reproach. I want to
be a woman of integrity to those around me and especially to those who are influenced by my example.

The big issues are easy to see, Lord. It's the small things,
the little missteps that concern me. These are the things
that erode my credibility with my family and friends,
things like accepting too much change at the checkout,
a personal story embellished, or a bit of gossip passed
along. I pray that You would help me keep a strong line
of integrity in my life.

Amen.

Whoever walks in integrity walks securely.
Proverbs 10:9 NRSV

MY PERSONAL PRAYER

*Integrity is the first step
to true greatness.*
Charles Simmons

Dear Father:

_____

_____

_____

_____

_____

_____

_____

Amen

*Our lives gradually become brighter and more beautiful as
God enters our lives and we become like him.*
2 Corinthians 3:18 MSG

Let integrity and uprightness preserve me, for I wait for You.
Psalm 25:21 NKJV

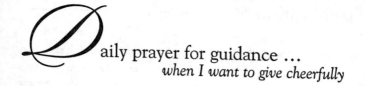

Daily prayer for guidance ...
when I want to give cheerfully

> *Your giving should be done in secret.*
> *Your Father can see what is done in secret,*
> *and he will reward you.*
>
> Matthew 6:4 NCV

Dear Heavenly Father,

You've given me so much. Thank You for everything. I enjoy it all, every last blessing. But, I don't want to greedily hold onto what You've given. I want to share it with others as cheerfully and generously as You've shared with me.

Help me hold onto my finances, possessions, and even my time, loosely. Nudge my heart toward generosity when there is a need You've enabled me to fill. I want to open my hands and home in love, not with the hope of admiration or recognition. Keep my pride in check. Guide me in knowing how to give wisely and, when possible, secretly.

Amen.

> *Don't give reluctantly or in response to pressure.*
> *For God loves the person who gives cheerfully.*
> 2 Corinthians 9:7 NLT

MY PERSONAL PRAYER

You can give without loving, but
you cannot love without giving.
Amy Carmichael

Dear Father:

_____

_____

_____

_____

_____

_____

Amen

Remember the words of the Lord Jesus, that He said,
"It is more blessed to give than to receive."
Acts 20:35 NKJV

The one who blesses others is abundantly blessed;
those who help others are helped.
Proverbs 11:25 MSG

Prayers to Encourage and Comfort the Soul

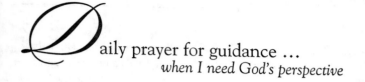

Daily prayer for guidance ...
when I need God's perspective

Look up, and be alert to what is going on around Christ—that's where the action is. See things from his perspective.

Colossians 3:2 MSG

Dear Heavenly Father,

What do You see when You look at me? At the people and situations in my life? I only see what's on the surface in real time. But You see to the core of the matter, to the heart of the person. And You see not only the here and now but also the past and the future.

I'm not able to see myself the way You do. My humanness just wouldn't be able to handle it. But I do ask that You would guide me as I strive to broaden my perspective, overcoming the limitations that often prevent me from being loving, kind, and forgiving. Help me to see past the human barriers I've constructed to see Your plan and purpose for me.

Amen.

It's in Christ that we find out who we are and what we are living for.
Ephesians 1:11 MSG

MY PERSONAL PRAYER

Prayer opens our eyes that we may see ourselves and others as God sees us.

Clara Palmer

Dear Father:

_____

_____

_____

_____

_____

_____

_____

Amen

It's important to look at things from God's point of view.
1 Corinthians 4:6 MSG

Keep your eyes open for GOD, watch for his works; be alert for signs of his presence.
Psalm 105:4 MSG

Prayers to Encourage and Comfort the Soul

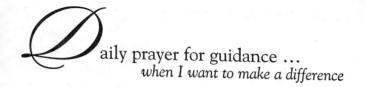

Daily prayer for guidance ...
when I want to make a difference

Pray that God will fill your good ideas and acts of faith with his energy so that it all amounts to something.

2 Thessalonians 1:11 MSG

Dear Heavenly Father,

Since I was a little girl, I've heard that one person can make a difference in this world. I want to do that, but it seems like my life is permanently stalled in the mundane. I feel like one big "blah." I hope it isn't too late for me, Lord.

I need Your guidance to know what's worth committing my time and effort to and what's worth crossing off my list. Help me plan my day, and my future, with Your big picture in mind. Then, please bless my efforts. Nothing I do will prosper if You're not part of it. Take the ordinary things I do and use them in extraordinary ways.

Amen.

Be strong and steady, always enthusiastic about the Lord's work, for you know that nothing you do for the Lord is ever useless.

1 Corinthians 15:58 NLT

MY PERSONAL PRAYER

God gives opportunities;
success depends upon the
use made of them.

Ellen G. White

Dear Father:

_____

_____

_____

_____

_____

_____

Amen

Serve the Lord enthusiastically.
Romans 12:11 NLT

May Jesus himself and God our Father, who reached out in
love and surprised you with gifts of unending help and confi-
dence, put a fresh heart in you, invigorate your work, enliven
your speech.
2 Thessalonians 2:16, 17 MSG

Prayers to Encourage and Comfort the Soul   131

For this new morning with its light,
Father, we thank Thee,
For rest and shelter of the night,
Father, we thank Thee,
For health and food, for love and friends,
For everything Thy goodness sends,
Father in heaven, we thank Thee.

Author Unknown

Daily Prayers of Praise ...

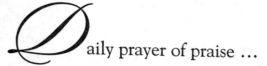# Daily prayer of praise ...

for life

*Celebrate God all day, every day, I mean,
revel in him!*

Philippians 4:4 MSG

Dear Heavenly Father,

Every breath I breathe is a gift from You. My beating heart, my pulsing blood, eyes that see and fingers that can caress a baby's cheek—these simple signs of life are gifts I take for granted every day. I thank You for my life, Lord.

I also thank You for the lives of those around me; my husband, my children, my parents, my siblings, my friends, my neighbors, all those You've placed around me. And Lord, I also thank You for the hope of eternal life—life in Your presence that will last forever. I praise You, Lord—the Giver of Life.

Amen.

*May the Lord continually bless you with heaven's blessings
as well as human joys.*

Psalm 128:5 TLB

MY PERSONAL PRAYER

Normal Day, let me be aware of
the treasure you are.

Mary Jean Iron

Dear Father:

_____

_____

_____

_____

_____

_____

_____

Amen

Your life is a journey you must travel with
a deep consciousness of God.
1 Peter 1:17 MSG

I will sing to the LORD as long as I live.
I will praise my God to my last breath!
Psalm 104:33 NLT

Prayers to Encourage and Comfort the Soul   135

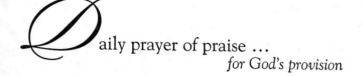

Daily prayer of praise ...
for God's provision

Give us the food we need for each day.
Matthew 6:11 NCV

Dear Heavenly Father,

It's a tradition to say a "blessing" at meals, to thank You for the food in front of us. But, Lord, I should be saying thank You continually throughout my day. You've provided me with so much more than just the food I eat, although without that single blessing, my life here on earth would come to an end.

Thank You for the home we live in, the ability to earn a living, the rain that waters the earth, and the sun that enables crops to grow. Thank You for the way You provide for my emotional needs, as well as my physical ones. You truly are a loving Father, abounding in generosity and goodness. I praise You, Lord—the Provision for all my needs.

Amen.

The LORD will guide you continually, watering your life when you are dry and keeping you healthy, too.
Isaiah 58:11 NLT

MY PERSONAL PRAYER

You will never need more than
God can supply.
J. I. Packer

Dear Father:

_____

_____

_____

_____

_____

_____

_____

Amen

I will send showers, showers of blessings,
which will come just when they are needed.
Ezekiel 34:26 NLT

Give me neither poverty nor riches!
Give me just enough to satisfy my needs.
Proverbs 30:8 NLT

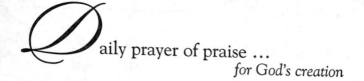

aily prayer of praise ...
for God's creation

The earth is the LORD's, and everything in it. The world and all its people belong to him.
Psalm 24:1 NLT

Dear Heavenly Father,

I know this world is imperfect, that evil has tainted some of Your precious creations. But, Lord, when I look at a snow-capped mountain range, consider the size and wonder of a whale, or hold a newborn baby in my arms, I cannot come away unmoved. Your creation humbles my heart. It reminds me of how big You are and how small I am—and yet how very much You love me.

Thank You for weaving such beauty into the tapestry of this world, for taking the time to make colors and cougars and kumquats. Your artistry draws me to worship You. I can see Your fingerprints on it all. I praise You, Lord—the Great Creator.

Amen.

Holy, holy, holy is the Lord of Hosts;
the whole earth is filled with his glory.
Isaiah 6:3 TLB

MY PERSONAL PRAYER

Were there no God we would be in this glorious world with grateful hearts: and no one to thank.
Christina Rossetti

Dear Father:

_____

_____

_____

_____

_____

_____

Amen

Christ is the one through whom God created everything in heaven and earth. He made the things we can see and the things we can't see.
Colossians 1:16 NLT

O LORD, what a variety of things you have made! In wisdom you have made them all.
Psalm 104:24 NLT

Prayers to Encourage and Comfort the Soul

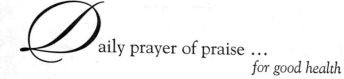

Daily prayer of praise …

for good health

Run to GOD! Run from evil!
Your body will glow with health, your very
bones will vibrate with life!

Proverbs 3:7, 8 MSG

Dear Heavenly Father,

I know my life is fragile. I know that the body You formed for me in my mother's womb will break down someday, allowing me to make the transition to a heavenly body that will never die. But right here, right now, I'm enjoying Your gift of good health.

Thank You for the body You've given me and for the miraculous way it functions day after day. Remind me not to take it for granted but instead to care for it as I would a glorious temple where Your presence dwells—which is exactly what it is. I praise You, Lord—the Great Physician.

Amen.

Keep my message in plain view at all times. Concentrate! Learn it by
heart! Those who discover these words live, really live; body and soul,
they're bursting with health.

Proverbs 4:21, 22 MSG

MY PERSONAL PRAYER

The most important prayer in the world is just two words long: "Thank you."

Dear Father:

_____

_____

_____

_____

_____

_____

Amen

A cheerful disposition is good for your health.
Proverbs 17:22 MSG

Lord, your discipline is good, for it leads to life and health.
Isaiah 38:16 NLT

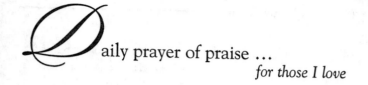

Daily prayer of praise …

for those I love

> *These God-chosen lives all around—*
> *what splendid friends they make!*
>
> Psalm 16:3 MSG

Dear Heavenly Father,

Thank You for the people You've placed in my life. I've come to love them all so deeply. And the way they've come to love me in return is one of the greatest joys I could ever have. It's taught me so much about what real love is like, not only about the joys, but the sacrifice. By loving others I've learned more about loving You.

Help me grow in those love relationships, to strengthen each one, to bring each one to a deeper, truer level. Protect those I love with Your mighty, compassionate hand and continue to draw us all closer to You. I praise You, Lord—my Loving Father.

Amen.

> *Thanking God over and over for you is not only a pleasure; it's a must.*
> 2 Thessalonians 1:3 MSG

MY PERSONAL PRAYER

When home is ruled according to God's Word, angels might be asked to stay with us, and they would not find themselves out of their element.

Charles Haddon Spurgeon

Dear Father:

_____

_____

_____

_____

_____

_____

Amen

We love because he first loved us.
1 John 4:19 NIV

Pursue faith and love and peace, and enjoy the companionship of those who call on the Lord with pure hearts.
2 Timothy 2:22 NLT

Prayers to Encourage and Comfort the Soul   143

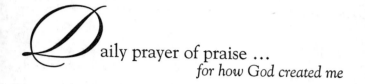

Daily prayer of praise …
for how God created me

Each of us is an original.
Galatians 5:26 MSG

Dear Heavenly Father,

Sometimes I'm so critical of the way You made me, comparing myself to others, striving for outer beauty without appreciating the unique work of art You've created in me. Yet, I know "I am fearfully and wonderfully made." Help me appreciate that gift more every day.

Thank You for the talents and abilities You've given me to use and enjoy in this life. Help me use them well. Continue to make me the woman You had in mind even before I was born. Bring out my own unique beauty in wonderful ways, even when wrinkles and gray hair form the outer frame for the masterpiece you call "me."

Amen.

I will praise You, for I am fearfully and wonderfully made;
marvelous are Your works, and that my soul knows very well.
Psalm 139:14 NKJV

MY PERSONAL PRAYER

*My Lord, I thank you
for having created me.*
Clare of Assisi

Dear Father:

_____

_____

_____

_____

_____

_____

Amen

*Our God gives you everything you need,
makes you everything you're to be.*
2 Thessalonians 1:2 MSG

*You know exactly how I was made, bit by bit,
how I was sculpted from nothing into something.*
Psalm 139:15 MSG

Prayers to Encourage and Comfort the Soul

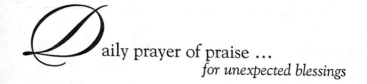

Daily prayer of praise ...
for unexpected blessings

I will open up the windows of heaven for you
and pour out a blessing so great you won't
have room enough to take it in!

Malachi 3:10 TLB

Dear Heavenly Father,

I'm overwhelmed with Your goodness! You never cease to amaze me with the surprisingly wonderful ways You choose to bless me. Thank You for how You've filled my heart with joy in a brand new way. You truly are a loving Father!

But, I don't want to stop at thanking You for the big miracles You bring into my life. I'm just as thankful for the small things: a baby's smile, a thoughtful gesture, a friend's encouraging word. And most special of all, are the unexpected blessings You send into my life: a brilliant sunset, a letter from an old friend, my teenager's "I love you." I praise You, Lord—the Giver of Blessings.

Amen.

May the LORD bless you and protect you.
May the LORD smile on you and be gracious to you.
Numbers 6:24, 25 NLT

MY PERSONAL PRAYER

*The more we count the blessings
we have, the less we crave the
luxuries we haven't.*
William Arthur Ward

Dear Father:

_____

_____

_____

_____

_____

_____

Amen

The godly are showered with blessings.
Proverbs 10:6 NLT

Happy indeed are those whose God is the LORD.
Psalm 144:15 NLT

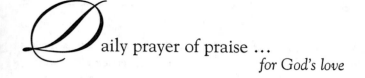

Daily prayer of praise ...
for God's love

If you are really wise, you'll think this over—
it's time you appreciated GOD's deep love.

Psalm 107:43 MSG

Dear Heavenly Father,

In the deepest part of my heart, I simply want to be loved. You've filled that need in a way that no husband, child, or friend ever could. You're not only my heavenly Father and sovereign Lord, You're my one true Love.

Your love has surrounded me every moment of my life. Even before I was aware of You, You were there, You loved me. Thank You for the countless ways You've expressed Your love to me, for filling my heart with what it longed for most. I rest each night and rejoice each day because You've promised to love me throughout eternity. I praise You, Lord—the Lover of my Soul.

Amen.

Christ died for us while we were still sinners.
In this way God shows his great love for us.

Romans 5:8 NCV

MY PERSONAL PRAYER

*We are all searching for the hug of
God, our ultimate true love.*
Carole Stewart McDonnell

Dear Father:

_____

_____

_____

_____

_____

_____

Amen

*Everything GOD does is right—
the trademark on all his work is love.*
Psalm 145:17 MSG

*When we obey him, every path he guides us on is fragrant
with his lovingkindness and his truth.*
Psalm 25:10 TLB

Prayers to Encourage and Comfort the Soul

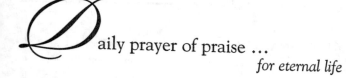

Daily prayer of praise ...
for eternal life

Jesus said, "I assure you, those who listen to my message and believe in God who sent me have eternal life."

John 5:24 NLT

Dear Heavenly Father,

The thought of eternal life is hard for my brain to comprehend. Everything I've known has a beginning and an end—everything except You. Thank You for Your gift of life that will never end, a life where my days will be as countless as the sand on the shore or the stars in the sky. May my gratitude be equally as infinite.

Never let me forget the sacrifice that made it possible for me to receive this gift—Jesus' death on the cross. The thought of spending eternity in the presence of a love like that is too great a gift to ever repay. I praise You, Lord—my Precious Savior.

Amen.

We who are still alive and remain on earth will be caught up in the clouds to meet the Lord in the air and remain with him forever.

1 Thessalonians 4:17 NLT

MY PERSONAL PRAYER

*Life is the childhood
of our immortality.*
Johann Wolfgang von Goethe

Dear Father:

_____

_____

_____

_____

_____

_____

Amen

*The troubles we see will soon be over,
but the joys to come will last forever.*
2 Corinthians 4:18 NLT

*Surely goodness and mercy shall follow me all the days of my
life; and I will dwell in the house of the LORD forever.*
Psalm 23:6 NKJV

Prayers to Encourage and Comfort the Soul   151

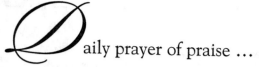

Daily prayer of praise ...

for heaven

> *Jesus said, "There are many rooms in my Father's home, and I am going to prepare a place for you."*
>
> John 14:2 NLT

Dear Heavenly Father,

I can't wait to see You face-to-Face, to fall before You in worship, to hear Your voice, to finally reach my true home in heaven. I don't know when that day will be, Lord. But You do. Prepare me for it. Help me not to fear death but to look beyond it, straight at You.

Thank You for creating a place where we can be together forever ... a place where there will be an end to tears and evil and injustice ... a place where angels dwell and hearts have been healed ... a place illuminated solely by the light of Your glory ... a place where I'll discover the true depth of my Father's love for His daughter.

Amen.

> *How we praise God, the Father of our Lord Jesus Christ, who has blessed us with every spiritual blessing in the heavenly realms because we belong to Christ.*
>
> Ephesians 1:3 NLT

MY PERSONAL PRAYER

We talk about heaven being so far away. It is within speaking distance of those who belong there.

Dwight L. Moody

Dear Father:

_____

_____

_____

_____

_____

_____

Amen

When we die and leave these bodies—we will have a home in heaven, an eternal body made for us by God himself and not by human hands.
2 Corinthians 5:1 NLT

He puts a little heaven in our hearts so that we'll never settle for less.
2 Corinthians 5:5 MSG

Prayers to Encourage and Comfort the Soul

Topical Reference Index

Prayer is the burden of a sigh,
The falling of a tear,
The upward glancing of an eye
When none but God is near.

James Montgomery

Every morning lean thine arms awhile
Upon the window sill of heaven
And gaze upon the Lord.
Then, with the vision in thy heart,
Turn strong to meet thy day.

Author Unknown